A Beginning-to-Read Book

A Visit to the Firehouse

by Mary Lindeen

NORWOOD HOUSE PRESS

DEAR CAREGIVER, The *Beginning to Read—Read and Discover* books provide emergent readers the opportunity to explore the world through nonfiction while building early reading skills. The text integrates both common sight words and content vocabulary. These key words are featured on lists provided at the back of the book to help your child expand his or her sight word recognition, which helps build reading fluency. The content words expand vocabulary and support comprehension.

Nonfiction text is any text that is factual. The Common Core State Standards call for an increase in the amount of informational text reading among students. The Standards aim to promote college and career readiness among students. Preparation for college and career endeavors requires proficiency in reading complex informational texts in a variety of content areas. You can help your child build a foundation by introducing nonfiction early. To further support the CCSS, you will find Reading Reinforcement activities at the back of the book that are aligned to these Standards.

Above all, the most important part of the reading experience is to have fun and enjoy it!

Sincerely,

Shannon Cannon

Shannon Cannon, Ph.D.
Literacy Consultant

Norwood House Press • P.O. Box 316598 • Chicago, Illinois 60631
For more information about Norwood House Press please visit our website at
www.norwoodhousepress.com or call 866-565-2900.
© 2016 Norwood House Press. Beginning-to-Read™ is a trademark of Norwood House Press.
All rights reserved. No part of this book may be reproduced or utilized in any form or by any
means without written permission from the publisher.

Editor: Judy Kentor Schmauss

Designer: Lindaanne Donohoe

Special thanks to the Chicago Fire Department, Engine #18

Photo Credits:

Phil Martin, cover, 3, 4-5, 6-7, 8-9, 10, 11, 14, 15, 16-17, 18-19, 22-23, 24, 25, 26-27, 28-29; Shutterstock 1; iStock, 12-13; Dreamstime, 20-21

Library of Congress Cataloging-in-Publication Data

Lindeen, Mary, author.
  A visit to the firehouse / by Mary Lindeen.
    pages cm. – (A beginning to read book)
  Summary: "Take a trip to a firehouse. Find out what firefighters wear, what equipment they use, and what they do when they're not fighting fires. See what's inside a firehouse and what happens when the alarm bell rings. This title includes reading activities and a word list"– Provided by publisher.
  Audience: K to grade 3
  ISBN 978-1-59953-693-4 (library edition : alk. paper)
  ISBN 978-1-60357-778-6 (ebook)
  1. Fire stations–Juvenile literature. 2. Fire fighters–Juvenile literature. 3. Fire extinction–Juvenile literature. I. Title.
TH9148.L56 2015
628.9′2-dc23
                                                              2014047628

Manufactured in the United States of America in Stevens Point, Wisconsin. 275N-062015

Who wears this helmet?
Who wears this coat?
Who wears these boots?

A firefighter wears these things.

Firefighters put out fires.

Firefighters work in a firehouse.

They keep their gear
in the firehouse.

They keep their tools in the firehouse.
Do you see the axes?

They use hoses to put out fires.
Do you see the hoses?

The fire engines are here, too.

It is time to wash this one!

Firefighters eat at the firehouse.

They cook for each other.

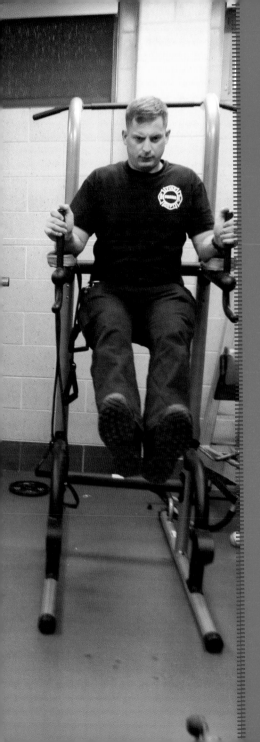

This firehouse has a gym.

The firefighters can exercise.

This is the fire chief.

He works in his office.

Some firehouses have a dog.

This dog lives at this firehouse.

There are beds
in the firehouse.

Firefighters can
sleep if they are
not at a fire.

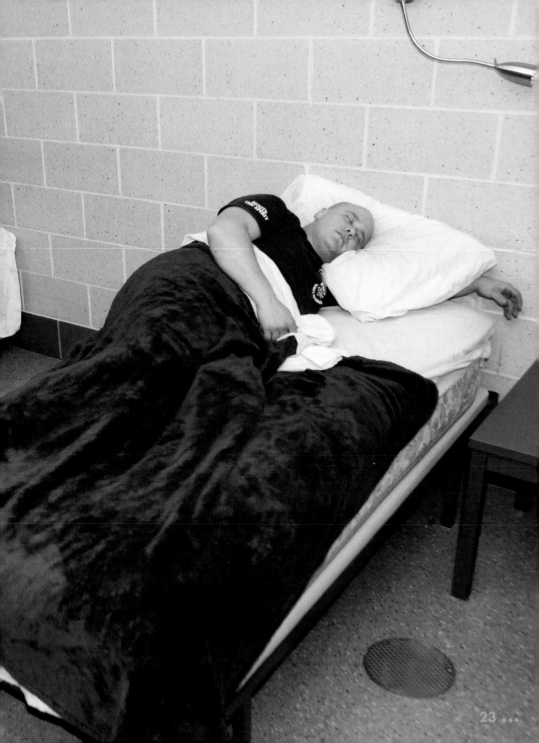

The alarm goes off! There is a fire!

The screen shows where the fire is.

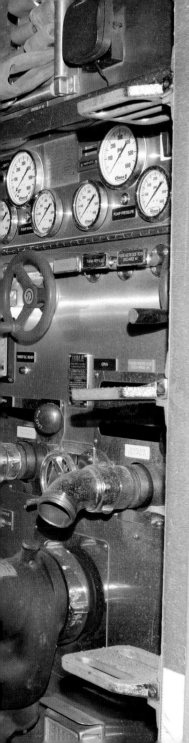

The firefighters have to be fast!

They put on their boots.

They put on their coats and helmets.

It is time to
go, go, go!

. . . READING REINFORCEMENT. . .

CRAFT AND STRUCTURE

To check your child's understanding of this book, recreate the following diagram on a sheet of paper. Read the book with your child, then help him or her fill in the diagram using what they learned. Work together to identify three cause-and-effect relationships in this book.

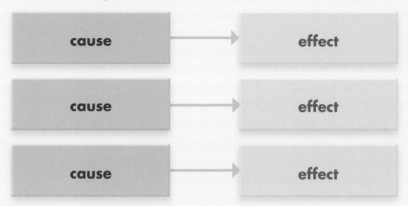

cause	→	effect
cause	→	effect
cause	→	effect

VOCABULARY: Learning Content Words

Content words are words that are specific to a particular topic. All of the content words for this book can be found on page 32. Use some or all of these content words to complete one or more of the following activities:

- Act out a content word and have your child guess the word. Switch roles.

- Help your child look for a smaller word within each content word. Make a list of the content words that have smaller words within them.

- Write each word and each definition on separate cards. Play a memory game by turning all cards face down and then turning them over to find matching pairs of words and definitions.

- Ask your child to sort the content words into two, three, or four categories of their own choosing. Then have him or her explain what the words in each category have in common.

- Have your child think of synonyms (words with similar meanings) or antonyms (words with opposite meanings) for as many content words as possible.

FOUNDATIONAL SKILLS: Regular plurals

Regular plurals are nouns that mean more than one person, place, thing, or idea. They are made by adding -s or -es to a noun. Have your child identify the regular plural words in the list below. Then help your child find regular plural words in this book.

ax/axes	hoses/hose	chiefs/chief
boots/boot	tool/tools	dogs/dog
engines/engine	bed/beds	pole/poles

CLOSE READING OF INFORMATIONAL TEXT

Close reading helps children comprehend text. It includes reading a text, discussing it with others, and answering questions about it. Use these questions to discuss this book with your child:

- What are two pieces of firefighting equipment?
- What would happen if firefighters didn't wear their gear?
- Why do firefighters sleep at the firehouse?
- Why do firefighters move fast when they hear the bell?
- Which room in a firehouse would be your favorite?
- Would you like to be a firefighter? Why or why not?

FLUENCY

Fluency is the ability to read accurately with speed and expression. Help your child practice fluency by using one or more of the following activities:

- Reread this book to your child at least two times while he or she uses a finger to track each word as you read it.
- Read the first sentence aloud. Then have your child reread the sentence with you. Continue until you have finished this book.
- Ask your child to read aloud the words they know on each page of this book. (Your child will learn additional words with subsequent readings.)
- Have your child practice reading this book several times to improve accuracy, rate, and expression.

••• Word List •••

A Visit to the Firehouse uses the 70 words listed below. *High-frequency* words are those words that are used most often in the English language. They are sometimes referred to as sight words because children need to learn to recognize them automatically when they read. *Content words* are any words specific to a particular topic. Regular practice reading these words will enhance your child's ability to read with greater fluency and comprehension.

High-Frequency Words

a	go(es)	it	show(s)	time
and	has	not	some	to
are	have	off	the	too
at	he	on	their	use
be	here	one	there	where
can	his	other	these	work(s)
do	if	out	they	you
each	in	put	things	
for	is	see	this	

Content Words

alarm	cook	fire(s)	hoses	tools
axes	dog	firefighter(s)	keep	wash
beds	eat	firehouse(s)	lives	wears
boots	engines	gear	office	
chief	exercise	gym	screen	
coat(s)	fast	helmet(s)	sleep	

••• About the Author

Mary Lindeen is a writer, editor, parent, and former elementary school teacher. She has written more than 100 books for children and edited many more. She specializes in early literacy instruction and books for young readers, especially nonfiction.

••• About the Advisor

Dr. Shannon Cannon is a teacher educator in the School of Education at UC Davis, where she also earned her Ph.D. in Language, Literacy, and Culture. She serves on the clinical faculty, supervising pre-service teachers and teaching elementary methods courses in reading, effective teaching, and teacher action research.